PIANO

Adventures®

by Nancy and Randall Faber

THE BASIC PIANO METHOD

CONTENTS

About the "Sightreading Stocking Stuffers"

A student's enthusiasm for learning Christmas music can become an opportunity to create enthusiasm for sightreading. In this book, each Christmas song is presented with short melodies, called "Sightreading Stocking Stuffers."

The "Sightreading Stocking Stuffers" are **melodic variations** of the carol being studied. Teachers will notice that the lyrics and rhythm patterns are from the carol. By drawing on these familiar rhythms, the student may effectively focus on interval reading and note reading.

The student should sightread one "stocking stuffer" a day while learning the Christmas song. Or, the stocking stuffers can be used as sightreading during the lesson itself.

The teacher may wish to tell the student:

> **Sightreading means "reading music at first sight."**
>
> When sightreading, music is not practiced over and over. Instead, it is only played once or twice with the highest concentration.

The following **3 C's** may help the student with sightreading:

CORRECT HAND POSITION
Find the correct starting note for each hand.

COUNT - OFF
Set a steady tempo by counting one "free" measure
before starting to play.

CONCENTRATE
Focus your eyes on the music, carefully reading the intervals.

Stuffing the Stockings

Each musical "gift" is an interval: **2nd**, **3rd**, **4th**, or **5th**.
Draw a line connecting each "gift" to the correct stocking.

Extra Credit: Play each "gift" on the piano using the fingering given.

We Wish You
a Merry Christmas

Traditional English

We wish you a mer-ry Christ-mas, we wish you a mer-ry Christ-mas. We wish you a mer-ry Christ-mas and a hap-py New Year. Good tid-ings we bring to you and your kin. Good tid-ings for Christ-mas, and a hap-py New Year!

Play the lowest C on the piano.

Teacher Duet: (Student plays *as written*)

Note: The words are familiar, but the **melodies have changed.**
The words will help you with the rhythm, but watch for these intervals—**2nd, 3rd, 4th, 5th**.

Sightread one "stocking stuffer" a day
while learning *We Wish You a Merry Christmas.*

Circle the stocking after sightreading!

("variations" for sightreading)

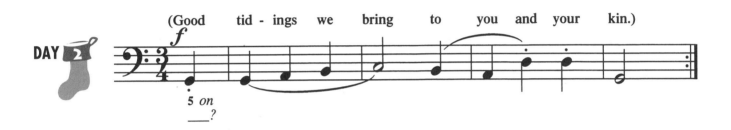

 DAY 5 Does each "stocking stuffer" above begin on **beat 1, 2,** or **3**? *(circle)*

 DAY 6 Write the letter names beside each note for **Day 2**.

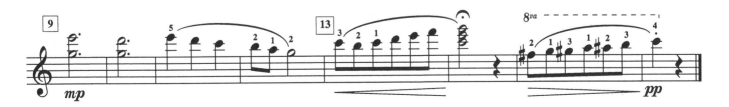

Go, Tell It on the Mountain

Bright swing tempo*

Traditional spiritual

Teacher Note: Students may play the eighth notes in a long-short pattern (♫ = ♩♪).

Teacher Duet: (Student plays *1 octave higher*)

Sightread one "stocking stuffer" a day
while learning *Go, Tell It on the Mountain.*

Circle the stocking after sightreading!

("variations" for sightreading)

DAY 1

3 on ___?

f (Go,   tell it on the moun - tain,   Go,   tell it on the moun - tain.)

DAY 2

mf (When I was a learn - er,   I   sought both night and day.)

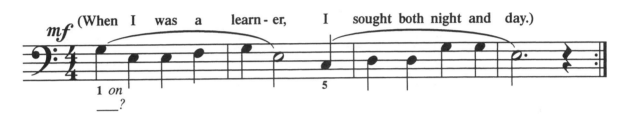

1 on ___?

Can you transpose to D major?

DAY 3

1 on ___?

mf (I   asked the Lord to   help me,   and   he showed me the   way.)

Can you transpose to G major?

DAY 4

f (Go,   tell   it on the moun - tain, that   Je - sus Christ_ is   born!)

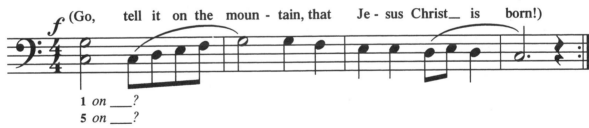

1 on ___?
5 on ___?

DAY 5   Can you sing the first 8 measures of
Go, Tell It on the Mountain without
playing the piano?

DAY 6   Circle all the **3rds** in the
"stocking stuffers" above.
(Hint: There are 10.)

Fine [9]   [13]   *D.C. al Fine*

p

The First Noel

Traditional English

Teacher Duet: (Student plays *1 octave higher*)

FF1139

Sightread one "stocking stuffer" a day
while learning *The First Noel*.

Circle the stocking after sightreading!

("variations" for sightreading)

DAY 1

(The__ first_____ No - el the an - gel did say.)

(Was to cer - tain poor shep- herds in fields where they lay.)

DAY 2

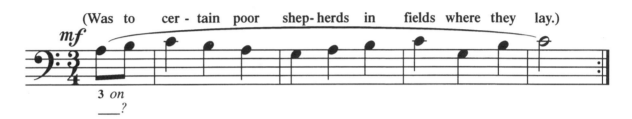

DAY 3

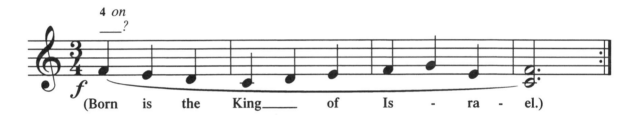

(Born is the King_____ of Is - ra - el.)

(In___ fields_____ where__ they lay keep - ing their sheep.)

DAY 4

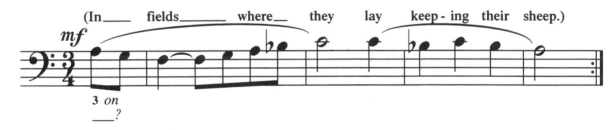

DAY 5

Write the counts "**1 - 2 - 3**"
under each beat for **Day 4**.

DAY 6

Circle this rhythm each time it
appears in the "stocking stuffers"
and in the carol, *The First Noel*.

Teacher Note: Some students may wish to substitute
the traditional ♫ ♩ ♩ rhythm for measures 1 and 2, 5 and 6, 13 and 14.

O Christmas Tree

Traditional German

Teacher Duet: (Student plays *1 octave higher*)

10

FF1139

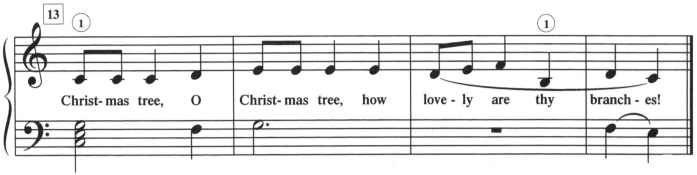

EVERGREEN STOCKING STUFFERS

("variations" for sightreading)

Sightread one "stocking stuffer" a day while learning *O Christmas Tree.*

Circle the stocking after sightreading!

DAY 1

Can you transpose to D major?

(O Christ - mas tree, O Christ - mas tree, how love - ly are thy branch - es!)

DAY 2

DAY 3

(They're green when sum - mer days are bright,)

Can you transpose to G major?

DAY 4

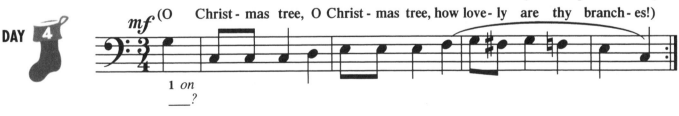

DAY 5 In the "stocking stuffers" above, put a ✔ above each measure with this rhythm:

DAY 6 How many times does the music of **measures 1-4** appear in *O Christmas Tree?*

Jingle Bells

Words and Music by
J. Pierpont

Merrily

Dash - ing through the snow in a one - horse o - pen sleigh;

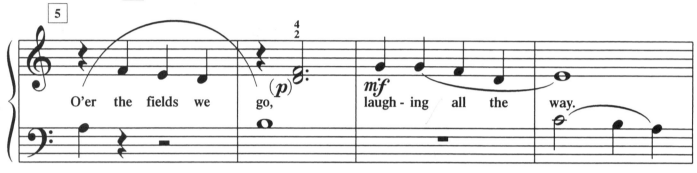

O'er the fields we go, laugh - ing all the way.

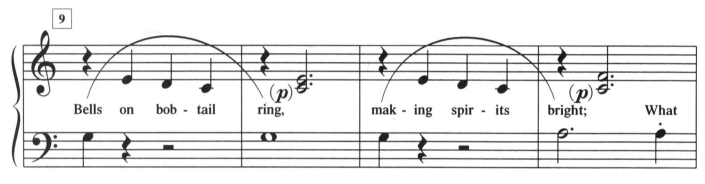

Bells on bob - tail ring, mak - ing spir - its bright; What

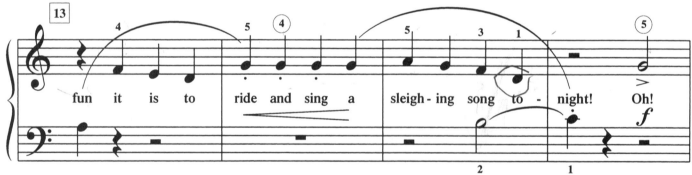

fun it is to ride and sing a sleigh - ing song to - night! Oh!

Teacher Duet: (Student plays *1 octave higher*)

FF1139

For piano solo: Continue with page 14 for an extended version of *Jingle Bells*.
For duet: End at measure 32.

Sightread one "stocking stuffer" a day
while learning *Jingle Bells*.

Circle the stocking after sightreading!

SLEIGHRIDE
STOCKING
STUFFERS

("variations" for sightreading)

Can you transpose to G major?

3 *on* ___?
1 *on* ___?

DAY 1

mf (Jin - gle bells, jin - gle bells, jin - gle all the way.)

DAY 2

mp (Oh, what fun it is to ride in (a) one-horse o - pen sleigh!)

2 *on* ___?

Name the position. ___

Can you transpose to A major?

3 *on* ___ #?
1 *on* ___?

DAY 3

f (Jin - gle bells, jin - gle bells, jin - gle all the way.)

Name the position. ___

Can you transpose to A major?

(Oh, what fun it is to ride in a one-horse o - pen sleigh!)

DAY 4

mf

1 *on* ___?

5

DAY 5

Write the 5 notes of **C Position**.
(Use whole notes.)

DAY 6

Write the 5 notes of **D Position**.
(Use whole notes.)

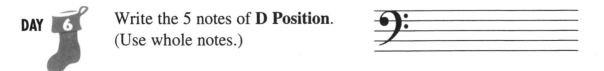

Silent Night

Words by Joseph Mohr
Music by Franz Grüber

Teacher Duet: (Student plays *1 octave higher*)

Sightread one "stocking stuffer" a day while learning *Silent Night.*

Circle the stocking after sightreading!

CHRISTMAS STOCKING STUFFERS

("variations" for sightreading)

DAY 1   Can you transpose to G major?

DAY 2   Can you transpose to D major?

DAY 3

DAY 4   Can you transpose to G major?

DAY 5   In *Silent Night,* circle each measure with this rhythm:

DAY 6   In *Silent Night,* put a ✔ above each measure that uses only notes of the **C chord.** (Hint: There are 9 measures.)

Pat-a-Pan

Moderately

Traditional French

mf (Willie's drum)

Wil - lie, *mp*

take your lit - tle drum; Rob- in, take your flute and come. When we

hear the tune you play, "Tu - re - lu - re - lu, pat - a - pat - a - pan." When we

hear the tune you play, how can an - y - one be

glum? *mf*

18

Sightread one "stocking stuffer" a day
while learning *Pat-a-Pan*.

Circle the stocking after sightreading!

("variations" for sightreading)

DAY 1

1 *on* ____?   5

mf

(Wil - lie,   take your lit - tle   drum; Rob - in, take your flute and   come.)

DAY 2

(When we   hear the tune you   play, "Tu - re - lu - re - lu,   pat- a- pat- a - pan.")

mp

2 *on* ____?   5

DAY 3

1 *on*
____?   4   1

mp

Can you transpose to A minor?

("Tu - re - lu - re - lu, pat- a- pat- a - pan. Tu- re- lu- re - lu, pat- a- pat- a- pan.")

Can you transpose to C minor?

DAY 4

mf

1 *on* ____?
5 *on* ____?

DAY 5

In the "stocking stuffers" above,
put a ✔ above each measure with
this rhythm:

DAY 6

Write **2nd**, **3rd**, **4th**, or **5th**
below each interval for **Day 4**.

Teacher Duet: (Student plays *as written*)

(Robin's flute)
8va throughout

5

mf

5

p

9 3

2

3

13 4   1   3

16

mf

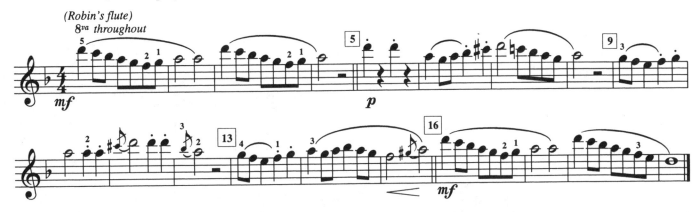

Christmas Music Calendar

Complete the music calendar for each day of December.

DEC. 1
Draw a pair of **8th notes** on the reindeer.

DEC. 2
Draw a **slur** under these notes.

DEC. 3
Draw the sign that means gradually louder.

DEC. 4
Draw a **G clef.**

DEC. 5
Draw an **F clef.**

DEC. 6
Draw a **quarter rest** on Santa's hat.

DEC. 7
= ___ beats

DEC. 8
Circle the interval formed by the stars.
2nd   3rd   4th   5th

DEC. 9
Draw the sign that means gradually softer.

DEC. 10
= ___ beats.

DEC. 11
Draw a **sharp** in the middle of the wreath.

DEC. 12
Draw a **half rest** on the sleigh.

DEC. 13
+ = ___ beats.

DEC. 14
Draw a **natural.**

DEC. 15
Draw a **whole rest** on the gingerbread man.

DEC. 16
Draw a **C chord.**

DEC. 17
Circle the interval formed by the stars.
2nd   3rd   4th   5th

DEC. 18
Draw a **G chord.**

DEC. 19
Put **staccatos** above these notes.

DEC. 20
Draw a **2nd** above this note.

DEC. 21
This music begins on beat ___ .

DEC. 22
Write the note names for these Christmas stars.

DEC. 23
Write the note names for these Christmas stars.

DEC. 24
Christmas Eve!
Decorate the tree with all the music symbols you can think of! (notes, rests, dynamics, clefs, etc.)

DEC. 25

Christmas Day!
Play your favorite Christmas songs!